ARTFUL DREAMING

Attention dear ones; a great source of wisdom is being revealed! Wewer Keohane's years of teaching dream work is little known outside our small mountain valley. Like a secret from a sage being given to the world, ***Artful Dreaming*** is a springboard to higher consciousness. Doing dream work is an endeavor that, earnestly pursued, can gently open the locked doors of our psyche and bring us closer to Beingness. We who have been guided by Wewer's years and years of study, experience and friendship are ecstatic that this gentle, simple, yet profound process of exploring the messages of your dreams is being brought to the rest of mankind. (Thank you, Wewer!)

ARTFUL DREAMING
A PRIMER FOR FINDING INSPIRATION
FROM YOUR DREAMS

First Edition Trade Paperback: 2009
Sections of this work were previously included in
The Dream Art Workbook, Copyright © Wewer Keohane, 1984-2009, and *Inspired by Dreams*, a lecture at Colorado Mountain College, and *The Art of Dreaming*, a lecture presented to the Association for the Study of Dreams, and a Book as Art publication.

Published by Oneirica Registered Trademark
OneircaArtRanch.blogspot.com

Cover Art: "Balance" by Wewer Keohane
Interior images are identified with the image.
If there is no ID, they are by Wewer Keohane.
Illustrations of Personal Symbols are by Wewer and/or Steve Keohane.
Author photograph by Jan Panico

Library of congress Cataloging-in-publication data has been applied for.
ISBN 1442137770   EAN-13 9781442137776

Created in the United States of America
10 9 8 7 6 5 4 3 2 1

ARTFUL DREAMING
A PRIMER FOR
FINDING INSPIRATION FROM YOUR DREAMS

WEWER KEOHANE, PH.D.

LOVE IS A VERB.

This book is dedicated to
my loving husband
and dream partner, Steve.

May your dreams
continue to bless
you with the
gifts of the
night —

Weaver

Gratitude makes sense of our past,
brings peace for today, and
creates a vision for tomorrow.

MELODY BEATTIE

ACKNOWLEDGMENTS*

I AM SO GRATEFUL FOR YOU:

STEVE KEOHANE - For simply being the best husband on the planet, digitizing of graphics, technical assistance, dinner every night, patience and unconditional love.

ISABEL — For nudging me to take a walk every day and for the simply joys you bring to my life.

DOUG EVANS — For your incredible patronage of my art, deep and loyal friendship, dedication to dream work and uplifting of spirit

STACI DICKERSON, LESLIE STOUPAS, & PAMA COLLÉ . If others had the depth we have in our friendships, the world would be a different place. No one surpasses your dedication to dream work.

DREAM GROUPS & DREAMERS— For allowing me to do the work I was put here to do. I am forever grateful for the privilege of sharing your dreams and for your belief in the depth of the work. I am fortunate that there are too many of you to name personally. I hope I can thank you in person once again.

HEARTS ON FIRE & THE ART GROUP — Without your enthusiasm, encouragement and friendships, would I have done this?

MIRIAM WOSK — For the inspiration your life and art gives me. You are a wonder.

ECKHART TOLLE — For A New Earth which changed my life in ways I never imagined.

NIGHT BLESSINGS — For dreams – those wonderful and mysterious gifts we are blessed with each night. Where would I be without you?

*Further acknowledgements are within the body of the book.

To become truly immortal,
a work of art must escape all human limits:
logic and common sense
will only interfere.
But once these barriers are broken,
it will enter the realms
of childhood visions and dreams.

GIORGIO DECHIRICO

ARTFUL DREAMING

A Primer for
Finding Inspiration from Your Dreams
Wewer Keohane, Ph.D.

Over ten years of dream work with Wewer Keohane has helped me learn to trust that through my dreams, I have answers to the challenges that show up in my life. This work is healing work, as my dreams situate me psychically in my life at deeper and deeper levels. *Artful Dreaming* has helped me access my own, unique creativity as well, encouraging me to forge my own imagination with the symbols of the unconscious, the boundless resource available to all of us through our dreams.

LESLIE L. STOUPAS, Writer/Artist

Table of Contents
Artful Dreaming
A Primer for Finding Inspiration from Your Dreams
by
Wewer Keohane, Ph.D.

What lies behind us and what lies before us are
tiny matters, compared to what
lies within us.

RALPH WALDO EMERSON

Dear Reader;

Thank you for purchasing this book. I hope it will inspire you to embrace your dream world and through that embrace you will find your life more joyful and your days more inspired.

Nothing beats the actual workshop experience, but I want to reach as many people as possible with the basic principles of my dream processes. Something happens during my work with others that allows a deep sense of knowing and safety and I hope my words convey the reverence I have for the work and for you, the dreamer. I want your life to be truly enhanced and for you to feel whole, alive and creative. I hope someday we will meet in person to share this journey.

I have been intensely interested in dreams since I was four. At that time, I had a paranormal dream that scared me so much I blocked remembering my dreams for about 7-8 years. It obviously had a great effect on me as I spent many decades of my life searching far and wide for places to gain knowledge about this mysterious aspect of myself. Symbol books never made sense to me. Jungian psychology is intriguing, but often too intellectual.

So I began to work with dreams in my own way, in my own time and style, keeping a journal since I was 13 years old, which included little sketches and poems which I used to make sense of the images.

In the early 1980s, while pursuing my doctorate, I met Dr. Montague Ullman. Monty, as I came to call him, has the same basic feelings about dreams as I do: They are intensely personal while at the same time universal. I began to work with his system of group process and he gave me permission to "do with it what moves you", and I have. I am indebted to every dreamer who has worked with me in this process. You have enriched my life.

My process sounds simple. I take every symbol of the dream, whether it is yours or mine, and I develop a metaphor for it that I honor as an aspect of myself. Further, I feel deeply into the dream, looking for the energy present....what I call the "felt sense", and I make art from that sense of energy, both written and visual. Creativity honors the dream.

In the following pages, I will teach you how to do the same, and how to combine the two for your own enjoyment and spiritual enrichment. You do not have to be an artist or writer to benefit from this process. You do have to have a desire to grow into your authentic self, which takes a bit of courage.

The results have led me into a deeper sense of self love and an ability to embrace my humanity, my shadow, my dark side, as well as the beautiful aspects of self that I have denied. Life is richer, more enjoyable, and centered around mystery, metaphor and creativity.

The paradox of dreamwork is that by taking all dream symbols personally one is able to take life impersonally. It is an immensely freeing experience. I hope you enjoy the journey as much as I am.

Wewer Keohane, Ph.D.
Provocateur of Art and Dreams

Always leave enough time in
your life to do something that
makes you happy, satisfied, even joyous.
That has more of an effect on economic well-being
than any other single factor.

PAUL HAWKEN

Expect your every need to be met,
expect the answer to every problem,
expect abundance on every level,
expect to grow spiritually.

EILEEN CADDY

CHAPTER ONE

FREQUENTLY ASKED QUESTIONS

?

In this section I answer the most frequently asked questions from the dreamers I have worked with over the last twenty five years. Email me via wewerart.com if you have a question I haven't answered.

The unconscious wants truth.
It ceases to speak to those who want
something else more than truth.

ANDRIENNE RICH

How Can I Remember My Dreams? (I don't know if I have any!)

Remembering a dream is like holding a bird.
Hold it too tight and you kill it.
Hold it too loose and it will fly away.

Obviously, if you want to be inspired by your dreams, you will have to begin remembering them. And, yes, you DO have them. Work in the dream lab has proven that most people have 4-7 dreams a night, whether they remember them or not.

Keep a pad of paper and a pen or pencil next to your bed, ready to use. When you notice you are awake, don't open your eyes. Stay in the state of "twilight imagery" and recall the images of the night, and your present feelings.

Adjust your body into the position it was in when you awakened. Begin writing in your journal: I know I had a dream last night. This is how I am feeling now.....
Often the dream will pop into your mind even if you thought you'd lost it. Many people begin remembering several dreams as they continue to write.

If you can't remember your dreams after trying the above method, drink a large glass of water before you go to bed

7

Make yourself write down or record the dream you recall in the middle of the night when you have to go the bathroom. (A pen light or small flashlight will be greatly appreciated by sleeping partners.) A voice activated recorder can be a great alternative to writing the dream.

As stated above, everyone dreams four to seven dreams a night, so be patient. Many alcohol-addicted people or people who are struggling to control their lives will not recall their dreams. If you are a very controlling person, take this as a message to relax. Allow this beautiful part of your life to surface and lessen your load. Be patient.

Before you go to sleep at night, say to yourself: "I have the courage to remember my dreams. I will have a dream tonight that I will willingly remember in the morning."

You can also ask your inner dreamer to help you with a problem you are having. As you go to sleep, concentrate on your desire to receive help. This is a form of incubation. Record the dream in the morning. I have had success with dreamers who have lost items being able to find them in the morning after incubating a question about their whereabouts.

In the weeks ahead, you will explore the many ways of benefiting from these wondrous mysteries we call dreams and you will be glad you have finally remembered them.

Many dreamers have found that once they commit to dream work, their recall of dreams increases. I believe the Dreamer Within is honored by our desire to remember and heed her messages, allowing better recall. Also, if you don't meditate, you might want to start. People who meditate have greater recall of their dreams, and many other desirable qualities.

Every time you don't follow your inner guidance, you feel a loss of energy, loss of power, a sense of spiritual deadness....follow that guidance directly and fearlessly.

SHAKTI GAWAIN

WHAT ARE THE BENEFITS OF DREAM WORK?

Dreams are windows to the soul, allowing us entry into the true nature of Self.

The benefits of dream work are vast. I speak a lot about the psychological benefits in the Inspired by Dreams section on literary arts (see Table of Contents). Dream work teaches us to let go of dualistic thinking. When we are not dualistic, we develop an unconditional awareness and we become more present. We drop victim behavior because we learn to own all parts of ourselves and we learn that what we project on others is our own shadow. We learn to observe (witness) ourselves......a first step to enlightened living. We benefit by waking up in the morning with a sense of wonder and mystery. And we certainly expand our sense of humor when we recall imagery that we have created in our dreams. When we learn to live with metaphor we drop the need to know why, a very freeing experience.

One of the benefits that is rarely talked about, but is huge for me and an impetus for this book, is the expansion of creativity. In meditation one morning I saw a thread running through my creative life that has been enhanced and guided by my dream life. People have often commented on my creativity, wondering how in the world I have come up with some of my ideas. Most of the time I am not sure how but many of my "inventions" have come straight from my dreams. This is such a gift and such a miracle of mystery, that I am constantly awed by its richness. Paying attention to my dreams has allowed my world to be vast and mysterious, fun and beneficial. I wake up with wonder and gratitude for the gifts of the night.

Also, I am amazed when I look back at dream sequences and notice how my life has progressed because of my work with inner symbols. Shoes have been a personal symbol as I've struggled to define my walk in life, feeling I "should" focus on one calling.

Twenty years ago I dreamed of opening a freezer door to see only a lighted bulb hanging and hearing Buddha direct his voice at me saying " Dharma, dharma, dharma." I have thought about that dream weekly over these years. Recently, the night after reading some poems I had written from that dream, I had a dream of being given three pairs of *identical* sandals. Each pair represents one of the dharmas (path, or walk in life). Finally, I saw that my combination of art, dreams

11

 and writing is my dharma, dharma, dharma. The sandals, with their heel (heal) straps and soles (soul), offer completion and a sense of relief that I have found my calling(s). Each equal to the other, represented by the identical qualities of the sandals.

There is also the benefit of learning to trust others, to be vulnerable, in a group dynamic. This enriches friendships, helps us to feel sane instead of isolated, and truly changes life experience. Please read the Inspired by Dreams section for more discussion of this topic.

I shut me eyes
in order to see.

PAUL GAUGIN

WHAT IS INCUBATION?

Incubation is the process of asking your "Dreamer Within" a question as you go to sleep at night in order to give possible focus to your dream. Some people ask practical questions, such as "where is my misplaced coat?". Others ask for spiritual guidance or ways in which to further their understanding of self. Relationship questions are popular.

As I have grown in my trust of dream work, I have asked more and more radical questions, such as: "Show me how to let go of all the unnecessary in my life." or "Show me how to embrace this dark aspect of myself."

I used to ask for the origin of my issues until I realized knowing the origin does not heal the issue. Now I ask more for guidance, grace, healing and creative inspiration.

A stubborn prospective client was quite skeptical about the validity of dream work until I suggested she go home and ask her dreamer within to find a lost item. She had been missing her camera for quite some time. As she went to sleep she asked to know the whereabouts of the camera. Upon waking she went straight to the linen closet and found it hidden under towels and sheets. She called me immediately and we began the process of dream work.

Although this practical use of dream incubation served her initially, she no longer limits her dream inspiration to finding lost objects!

. The god of dream incubation, Asklepios, is the wounded healer archetype. Originally, incubation was used for healing illness. When the dreamer asked for healing, the dream delivered.

I believe this to be true. Just recalling a dream creates a sense of healing for the dreamer. And, whether we are attuned to our dream world or not, the dream is moving us forward in our lives.

When inward tenderness
finds the secret hurt,
pain itself will crack the rock
and AH! let the soul emerge.

RUMI

WHAT DO YOU MEAN WHEN YOU TALK ABOUT DREAMS AS MIRRORS?

One of the most powerful ways to work with dreams (the best way, as far as I'm concerned), is as a mirror of self. If we take every symbol in our dream as a metaphor for a part of ourselves, we will learn an immense amount about our subconscious world.

For instance, instead of my mother being my mother in my dream, my mother is the part of myself that is like my mother. This will help us own all the disowned parts of ourselves (shadow) and become atoned (at one with self).

I believe in this way of working with dreams, and I know how difficult it is from personal experience. For instance: Many years ago I had a dream about a man I had just met and become quite infatuated with. In the dream, we were taken into a basement full of bones by some beautiful angels. On the mantel was a candlestick made of two intertwined pieces. The candle was lit and the angels said to me: this is you.

At this time I had been working with dreams for at least twenty years and I broke my own rule. I decided this was one of those rare dreams that wasn't metaphoric! Hah! I decided I was supposed to be with this man. After all.....Angels! Can you imagine?

Almost two years later, I had a similar dream and it, along with the two very hard years of dating this man, helped me realize that the part of me that I wanted to believe was this man was indeed a disowned part of myself. He represented my anger. I began to own my own anger and to do my best to love the angry part of myself. Not long after, I was able to release myself from the relationship.

In another dream, a woman dreamed her husband was having an affair with her best friend. She knew, when she awakened, that this was not true. Rather than accuse her husband, she asked herself: How am I betraying myself? This led her toward a renewed dedication of self nurturing.

Own your dreams. See the dream as a *mirror of the aspects of your psyche.* This will help you to be accountable in your waking life and you will become free from any victim energy you may be carrying. It is *not* easy. It *is* worth it. Your life will change dramatically when you begin dropping blame and owning your own projections on other people. Doing this process in your dreams will lead to new waking behavior.

As my husband says: We are all multi personalities with a delusion of continuity!

Begin by writing down the characteristics of the person in the dream. Or describe the person out loud to yourself or a dream partner. Be honest, even if you know the person represents parts of yourself you'd rather not own.

Remember, you may need to own beautiful aspects of self you have denied.

One of the most touching examples of disowning our beauty came when a dreamer was describing to the group her Aunt who had mysteriously appeared in her dream. I asked her to describe the Aunt as if I was an alien and knew nothing about her. As she told us how elegant her Aunt was, she began crying. We asked, "What's coming up for you?" She said, "I'm having trouble owning that she is part of me." We assured her we all see her as elegant. It was touching to witness her awakening to her own beauty and elegance.

Over time this process becomes second nature. In the beginning it is quite difficult. Be patient and gentle with yourself.

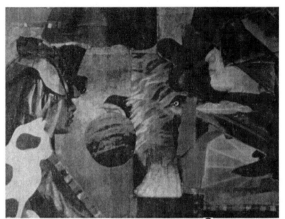

Synthesis: When the King & Queen Unite © Wewer Keohane

WHAT IS MY SHADOW?

May your darkness
lead you to your light
and your stillness
to dancing.
T.S. Eliot

Jung referred to the disowned parts of ourselves as our Shadow. You may refuse to own your beauty or your greed, either could be considered the shadow side of yourself. In our dreams, the shadow aspects reveal themselves to us through the mirrors (see previous pages) of our dream symbols. The dream helps us to integrate these parts of ourselves that we refuse to see in ourselves, but are usually quick to see in others. CLUE: Whatever you criticize in another is most likely your shadow material, not theirs. Likewise, if you have someone on a pedestal, you might not be owning your radiance.

In our society many people pretend that evil only exists outside themselves. Unless we own the parts of ourselves that we are projecting on others, we will never be whole. Exploring our dreams can help us embrace the parts of ourselves we have been judging so harshly. This will help us drop judgment of others.

Auden said it beautifully:

Love your crooked neighbor
With your own crooked heart.

Vanity (detail) © Wewer Keohane

This is the work of the shadow: to help us see that we are many-faceted beings and all our facets need love and attention. If I am greedy, how is it serving my needs? If I fill the needs in another way, such as giving myself more attention, will the greedy part of me be satisfied and feel loved? The tendency is to try to "figure out" why I am greedy. I suggest dropping the need to know why. Instead, feel into how it feels to be greedy and how it would feel to be generous. You might soon attract generous people and fewer people with scarcity problems. Look for the metaphors in the dream that represent greed or its opposite and embrace both.

Remember, dreams, like art, fall flat without shadow. Shadow is what gives us perspective and dimension.

Years ago I began a series of dreams in which I was embracing a murderer. I knew I was developing a new relationship with my shadow with these dreams. After months and months of bringing my shadow aspects to consciousness, I had the following dream:

I am in a beautiful grassy green meadow with a bowl shape to it. I am on the edge of the bowl and am holding hands with people who spiral around and around the edge of the bowl into its center. When I see that everyone has held hands I begin to sing "From you I receive, to you I give, together we share, from this we live." Everyone in the spiral began singing and we sang and sang. After the singing I realized that these were all previously competitive Mafia families and they had now come together as one. The men held out their pistols and they became baseball card-like relics, never to be used again in warfare.

This dream felt like a miracle to me. Could my previously warring aspects be in harmony? That is what the dream

21

message felt to be to me. I felt very peaceful and delighted that maybe I was going to be free of some old internal conflicts and that I had owned some pretty dark aspects of my shadow.

Years before I had this dream, my fears and judgments would have awakened me from this dream the moment I realized I was with the Mafia, but I now see that this is a metaphor for my inner mafia, and the wars are over. I have actually developed love for my dark side.

This can only happen when we own our shadow material. This reminds me of my favorite poem by Antonio Machado.

In 1991, at a Brugh Joy retreat, I was fortunate to hear poet David Whyte orate this poem. He kept repeating it and repeating it. I was at the retreat with my husband, Steve. We hadn't been married long, and I had been praying and meditating on letting go of the past so that our future would be possible together and not hurt by our old relationship baggage. As David Whyte so beautifully recited this poem, I began to cry and I was swept with a self forgiveness that has stayed with me today. All the aspects I had judged about relationship were owned and forgiven. It was a waking experience of shadow ownership. It still puts fire in my heart to remember it, and it is impossible to verbalize the felt sense of the healing.

Here is the magical poem that serves as a metaphor to me of the healing power of dreams:

**Last night, as I was sleeping
I dreamt – marvelous error! –
that I had a beehive
here inside my heart.
And the golden bees
were making white combs
and sweet honey
from my old failures.**
Antonio Machado

Nocturne © Wewer Keohane
Inspired by Machado's poem.

Note: Steve and I will celebrate our 18th anniversary in 2009. Thank you Brugh, Antonio and David!

WHAT IS A NIGHTMARE?

If you are pursued by an ogre in a dream and you
become the ogre, the nightmare disappears. You
own the energy that is invested in the demon.
Then the power of the ogre is no longer outside,
aberrant, but inside where you can visit.   Fritz Perls

A nightmare is simply a dream that is trying to get your attention. If I am blocking information the Dreamer Within has about my waking ego and situation, a dream with adversarial elements will confront the ego and become a nightmare. When I change my attitude and want to sleep through adversarial situations for dream resolution, I have decided not to block the dream, due to fear, and I will not awaken.

In other words, nightmares in adults are dreams which get blocked by the waking ego and create an awakening. The awakening is asking for attention in the waking life. Work on your nightmare (and recurring) dreams first.

I have *never* worked with a nightmare that didn't turn out to be a powerful and *positive* message in the end. Some people are being encouraged by their dream analysts to control their nightmares. **DON'T!!** Instead, go into the feeling and ask yourself what the metaphors are saying to you. If you can, ask a question of the perpetrator during the dream and listen for the answer. It will only be a short term relief if you turn the demon into a flower. Instead, ask the demon what he wants and go from there.

Here are some examples:

I worked with a wonderful woman who had had a recurring nightmare for almost fifty years, causing chronic insomnia. Yes.....she had suffered most of her life with this! She had been scared to feel into the meaning, and had not been able to find help. With encouragement and a safe place to do the work, she finally took a look. The dream turned out to be very positive. She could have lived without her fear of going to sleep for many many years had she felt into the dream sooner.

S. dreamed that there was an ogre circling her bed every night. It was a scary looking creature and she was afraid it was going to do her harm. Her insomnia was due to her fear of his visitation in her dream state. I began asking her questions such as, when did this dream begin; has the feeling about the ogre changed over the years, etc. This dream began when S.'s parents divorced and she was a very young girl. This was a clue and I asked her if she could ask either of her parents about that time. Unfortunately, her parents were both deceased, but S. had an aunt and she called her. It turns out that after her parents divorced, S.'s Mom would not let her Father see her *except* when S. was sleeping. He was allowed to look in her bedroom window.....that was it! At 55 years old, this was a total revelation to S. After further working with the dream, the positive outcome was this: Rather than S. feeling abandoned by her Father as she had throughout her life, she developed great compassion for him and felt great love from him. It took some work to forgive her Mom, but with further dreams, she was able to do this as well. What she realized was that the "ogre" was not there to scare her, he just wanted to be close to her. She has never had the dream again.

Another dreamer dreamt of a "horrible bear". The bear chased her night after night in different situations. Someone recommended she turn the bear into flowers. Amazingly, she was able to do this, but it only worked for a night. The bear returned. I encouraged her to challenge the bear. The next time the bear was in her dream he was chasing her from her boat into the woods, not allowing her to have the picnic she wanted. She remembered she was supposed to confront the bear so on the chase, she turned and yelled at it, "what do you want?" The bear turned into a puddle. She tasted the puddle. It was alcohol.

She woke up and believed the bear was her alcoholic Father and this allowed some further work. Eventually, she was able to own that the bear was her own alcoholism, which was consuming and torturing her. She grieved this and along with continued dream work, got help from AA and she has never been confronted by the bear again.

Even nightmares can be sweet if we listen wholeheartedly to their message for us. Have courage and look at how the nightmare might resemble your waking life. This can be a major step toward inner peace. I have seen it cure post traumatic stress disorder, and other disabling behaviors. When I begin work with a new client, I always ask to hear nightmares and recurring dreams first as they usually hold the information that will guide us to issues most needing attention.

WHICH OTHER BOOKS SHOULD I READ?

There are many good books on the market to experience even more in-depth information about dream work. Two of the most inspiring are Alex Lukeman's **What Your Dreams Can Teach You** and Henry Reed's **Getting Help from your Dreams** (both out of print, but available on amazon.com).

Any books by Marion Woodman or Robert Moss will be a feast for your psyche, as will **Joy's Way** by Brugh Joy and **A New Earth** by Eckhart Tolle. These are not specifically about dreaming, but these authors are able to awaken the energy I call "felt sense" needed to fully explore the depth of our dreams.

Whatever you do, DO NOT buy a symbol book. The dreamer is the author of the dream. Therefore, symbols will be personal, even when they have a universal or archetypical theme. For this reason, I have an A to Z index in the back of this book for you to record your own symbolism, and that of any group members you may feel are appropriate for you. Remember, we have similar emotions but different history, which will affect the meaning of our symbols and metaphors. For instance, a dog saved my life when I was a child. If you were bitten by a dog, you will have a different emotional charge than I will have when we dream of dogs, even though universally a dog may represent loyalty.

Rather than getting a symbol book, study mythology, which will give you a universal picture of how symbolism presents itself in our dreams.

Please read **Memories, Dreams, Reflections** by Carl Jung, and any of his other works. They are truly inspiring.

For the literary artist in you, try Naomi Epel's **Writer's Dreaming.**

Drawing on the Right Side of the Brain is the best instructional art book on the planet, and will change more than your ability to draw. It will help you see, truly see.

Just remember to Trust Your Feelings and Be Courageous and you will discover the meaning of your own dreams. In the following pages there are many more tips for mining the gold of your dreams.

The center
that I cannot find
is known to my
unconscious mind.

W.H. Auden

CHAPTER TWO

WORKING ALONE

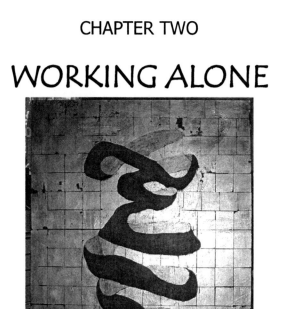

Mind over Matter © Wewer Keohane

Dreams are windows to the soul, allowing us
entry into the true nature of Self.

Be really whole and
All things will come to you.

LAO-TZU

DREAM ANAGRAM

DREAM with a desire to remember your dreams. Discover the part of your life that does not live in denial. Touch divinity. Touch darkness. Say to yourself: "I will dream tonight and have the courage to remember". Dedicate yourself to decoding your dream. Dialogue with the dream and its symbols and characters.

REMEMBER and record your dream. Read your dream aloud if you've written it, listen to it if you've recorded it. Remember, the dream reflects who we are, our authentic self, our truth.

ENCOURAGE your feelings to surface. Notice emphasis. Have the courage to encourage your grieving process to show itself. Energize your own healing. BE. Let your heart run the show, not the Ego.

ASSOCIATE with and own the symbols and characters. How do you feel being them? Do they remind you of anything in waking life? Make ART from your dreams.
ACTIVATE YOUR CREATIVITY!! BECOME AWAKE!!!

MAKE metaphors for the symbols, characters, feelings and incidents. Melt into the mystery and wonder – what a way to start the day! Meld the masculine and the feminine inside yourself into a sacred marriage within. What do you see in the mirror of the dream?

INCUBATE your dreams to resolve conflict, process loss, answer questions, and encourage creativity and spiritual awakening. Be immediate! How does each image make you feel? Prevent insanity! Be Inspired!

NAME your dream with a title. Name your roles and the roles of others in the dream. Accept the numinous connection within your dreams – a power and wisdom beyond our own – the "felt sense".

GROW into an integrated person whose external and internal lives are congruent- one. Dreams make us awake. Remember, the voice of the great creator.....the great consciousness... speaks through the dream. Gently ask and listen. You WILL get answers. Go for it!

Come to the edge, he said.
But we are afraid, they said.
Come to the edge, he said.
They came.
He pushed them.
And they flew!
G. Apollinaire

Welcome to the edge.

Life shrinks and
expands in proportion
to one's courage.

ANAIS NIN

AN EXERCISE

1. Take a short recent dream and write it down. (Note: later, you can condense dreams to paragraphs, or make time to work with longer dreams.)
2. Circle every noun in your dream and on the left of the next page, make a column of the nouns.
3. At the right of each noun, write the first thing that comes to your mind. (Jung called this free association.)
4. On the next page, write the original dream over with the new word or phrase in the original noun's place. After each new word or phrase, add the phrase "part of myself". This exercise will not only help you understand your dream by yourself, it will give you a first hand example of the power of ownership through mirroring.

Here is an example:

The dream: I am about to give a lecture in a museum about one of my paintings. The curator tells me I have a phone call. There is an old fashioned black phone on a pedestal. I pick up the receiver. Andy Warhol is calling from heaven.

Nouns	free associated words
I	the painter
lecture	serious talk
museum	history
paintings	acts of creation
curator	protector or art
call	message
phone	tool of communication
pedestal	lofty
receiver	conduit for communication
Andy Warhol	dead wacky artist
heaven	spiritual world

After the exercise, the dream reads as follows:

The painter part of myself is about to give a serious talk part of myself in a history part of myself about one of my acts of creation parts of myself. The protector of art part of myself tells me I have a message part of myself. The old tool of communication part of myself is on a lofty part of myself . The painter part of myself picks up the conduit for communication part of myself. It is the dead wacky artist part of myself calling from the spiritual world part of myself.

38

With a little work, I am able to feel that the dream is telling me that I had become far too serious (lofty) about my art and it was appropriate to be wacky! The wacky part of me had died. This created a major shift in my work and I am grateful to my internal metaphor of Andy. He helped me get off my pedestal and to have fun.

If writing "part of myself" feels awkward to you, try writing "my" before the new word and "self" after it. This reads a little differently and some may find it more easily absorbed by the ego. For instance, instead of "the painter part of myself" the dream would read "my painter self". Either way will get you to a new meaning if you use the free associated words.

Now.....you give it a try.

Dream Worksheet Summary

1. Write a short dream or summarize a long dream into a paragraph.
   Write what you think the dream is about before doing the work.

2. Circle all nouns (and pronouns if you wish), then list them in a column.

3. Word associate – write what first comes to your mind for each word and write that word across from word in column (it does not have to be a noun or just one word). Allow your intuition to play a part in this.

4. Replace all circled nouns, etc., with the new word(s), adding "part of myself" after each one. OR.....put "my" before each word and "self" after.

5. Read "new" dream to yourself a few times.

6. Write the new meaning in a way you understand it. It may take a few attempts.

7. Continue working this way until you receive an "ah ha".

8. Dreams often have a felt sense that is verbally indescribable, as can poetry. (Dreams are poetry!)

Read the poem below and you will feel what I am trying to convey. You will *feel* what the poem means, but it will be impossible to verbally describe what you are feeling. This is how it can be with a dream. Open your heart to the dream's message as you open your heart to this poem.

All things
are too small
to hold me,
I am so vast

In the Infinite
I reach
for the Uncreated

I have
touched it,
it undoes me
wider than wide

Everything else
is too narrow

You know this well,
you who are also there

Hadewijch II - Thirteenth Century Flemish Beguine

41

All the arts we practice
are apprenticeships.
The big art is our life.

M.C. RICHARDS

CHAPTER THREE

INSPIRED BY DREAMS:
VISUAL ART

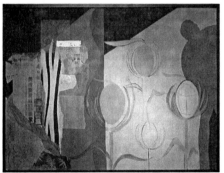

Winged Deer © Wewer Keohane

Artists who seek perfection
in everything are those who
cannot obtain it in anything.

E. DELACROIX

After many years of studying dreamwork, I began to draw and paint my dreams. My healing and growth took a huge leap. None of the scholastic work I had done could match what began to happen when I honored my dreams with tactile creations.

My main quest as an artist is the revelation of the unconscious through creativity.....making the invisible visible. I want to tap that resource and help others tap it as well. Fame is of little importance. If it happens, it was meant to be. I am not, in the meantime, out to please others with my art. I am on a quest to find my authentic self. Welcome aboard! Let dreams be your muse also. They are our Rosetta stones. What a way to find the Holy Grail!!

Never have I believed that anyone can know the meaning of the dream better than the dreamer. Therefore, I have never called myself an analyst. Instead, I am a coach, asking questions to guide dreamers to their deepest understanding of their dream, and encouraging them to express these night symbols through the arts. I do not encourage intellectual understanding, but a "sense of knowing", or "felt sense" that only comes from feeling. Understanding doesn't heal; feeling does.

Doing dream work with a client resembles going to the movies with a trusted friend and discussing the movie's meaning, effect and relevance on your lives. You are peers. Neither is the authority. Each view is honored.

So.....when working with your dreams as inspiration for art, remember to feel and honor the energy of the dream. Through this process you will come to know yourself and hopefully love yourself for all that you are. Making art from your dreams gives you the courage and tools to be authentic. I hope you will allow your dreams to awaken your artist within, as this alone is a very healing process.

For echo is the soul of the voice
exciting itself in hollow places.

MICHAEL ONDAATJE

TWO DIMENSIONAL EXERCISES

Dreams are incredible inspiration for visual art. Take a break from talking about self discovery and make art from your metaphors for some fun. Let the unique voice of your dream become your visual voice through art. You can be sure that this will be **your** visual voice, and yours alone.

Begin by journaling your dream. Just start writing about how you feel, what the dream reminds you of, some childhood memory or what happened yesterday. Take some quirky image from the dream and sketch it. This can not only get you started in a new creative manner, but it makes the dream easier to find in your dream journal.

Dream journal entry, "Flame of the Heart" © Pama Collé

Draw a dream right here!!!!

COLLAGE

Collage is a great way for anyone to translate their dream into visual imagery. Here's the best way I've found to get the most from the power of the dream through collage:

1. Collect a large pile of used magazines and a kitchen timer.
2. Choose a dream to work with. (Yours or someone else's.)
3. Gather scissors, glue stick (I like the ones from 3M that allow you to pick up and move imagery before finalizing position of the image).
4. You need at least 45 minutes to do this exercise.
5. Find a substrate of either paper or hardboard, whatever size you like to work with. 11 x 14" is a great size.

Now, "redream" the dream in your head, feeling deeply into its message. The work is in three segments.

1. Spend fifteen minutes going through the magazines finding imagery or color that FEELS like the dream. Literal images are fine, but the feeling of the dream is what you want to convey. Rip the images out and put them in a pile.

2. Spend fifteen minutes cutting the imagery away from the page that you ripped out and begin placing the pieces on your substrate.

3. Spend fifteen minutes pasting the imagery into a collage that feels right to you. Don't think too much. Enjoy the process. Fill spaces in with paint or colors if you like.

4. You can stop here and admire your collage. I suggest putting it somewhere you can see it every day for at least a week so you can meditate on it.

5. Further fun can be had if you scan the collage and play with it on your computer.

6. For artists who are looking for material for paintings and their fine art, taking the collage and using it as a sketch book works great. I translate my collages into mixed media pieces, photograms, and paintings.

7. If this process works for you, buy yourself a sketchbook that is for dream collages only. This will catalog your dream series and give you years of inspiration for further artistic endeavors.

CARVING & PRINTING

An all time favorite dream-honoring creation is the carving and print process. You will need a linoleum cutter, a block of carving rubber or a large eraser to carve, a bone folder or a Popsicle stick, tracing paper, pencil, inkpad, watercolors or color markers, old phone book or scrap paper and sketchbook.

First, draw your dream symbol in your sketchbook to the size of your carving rubber. Then, trace the drawing onto tracing paper. Turn the tracing paper upside down on the carving rubber and rub it with the side of your bone folder or Popsicle stick until the graphite image transfers on to the rubber.

Read the directions that come with your linoleum cutter. The kit usually comes with five blades and you want to start with the smallest blade, cutting along the graphite line of your image. The main trick is to hold the rounded part in the palm of your hand and guide it rather than push it.

Below you will see two carvings of the same image, one called an "outie" and one called an "innie".

"Balance" (outie)   "Balance" (innie)

In both the outie and the innie, you carve away what you *don't* want to print. In other words, what you see as white in the prints above was carved away. Obviously, in the outie, I used a larger blade than I used for the innie.

As you carve, do some sample prints on the pages of an old phone book or scrap paper by pressing your carving into the inkpad or brushing your carving with watercolor, or drawing on your carving with markers. Keep carving until you are happy with the print. Watercolor will give you a soft image without hard lines, whereas an ink pad will give you very defined lines. Markers are somewhere in between.

Make a series of final prints in your sketchbook and then dream journal. Make a packet of greeting cards with your image on the front.

As you get comfortable with this process, you can enlarge your format by buying larger and larger carving rubber and expanding from a symbol to a whole dream scene.

Here is a great example of the process I teach in my Artful Dreaming workshops as done by Leslie Stoupas. Thank you Leslie.

Take a dream that has meaning to you, choose a symbol, carve the symbol, make further art with the symbol (see cover of her book in 3-D section):

The dream: I am living in a tent city and the residents are having some kind of party. A black panther strolls through the tents, and I am intent on following him. He is elusive, but I can see his tail as he goes around corners. Finally, I come face to face with the panther and when I do, I find myself having to stand taller to face him. However, I quickly realize that he is not a threat but has come to deliver a message to me.

The work: This dream took place at a time when I was re-engaging with my creative life as a necessary expression of an authentic self. The panther in the dream took on the significance of that emergent self: elusive, powerful, mobile, knowledgeable, and in the end, able to encourage my ability to stand tall in my own  life. I created the symbol from the dream as mimicry of the panther's tail, the image I chased through the dream to bring me to myself. I used the symbol in artwork and as a reminder that underneath all the temporary situations in life (signified by the tent

53

city, an impermanent state of life), I have the knowledge to bring me back to my sense of self.

Take one of the collages you have done and translate it into a carving.   You are on your way to being an authentic mixed media artist.

Here are some examples of dream collage, painting, and computer "sketching".

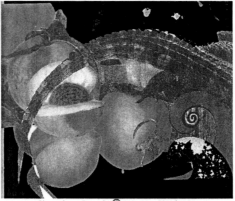

Cherokee Peach © Wewer Keohane

Art from another dreamer's dream:

Leslie's PCV dream © Steve Keohane

Attic Dream © Lynne DeNio

I was giving two friends, a woman and a man, a tour of my new home. It was a large old house with many rooms. In particular, I wanted them to see the attic. As we approached the attic door we could heard a baby crying. I opened the attic door to reveal a huge, gray, dusty warehouse room full of boxes and cobwebs. In a distant corner, dust-flecked light filtered in through a few small windows. I looked for the source of the crying (which had stopped) and in the corner illuminated by the light rays, I saw a tiny infant sleeping snugly in a blanket. The baby was not in distress; in fact the baby was perfect. I lifted the baby in my arms and felt a sense of serenity that the child would be safe. At this point, the dream ended abruptly.

At the time of this dream I was reading "The Artist's Way" by Julia Cameron (and I had just taken Wewer's Dream Intensive). Julia often encouraged nurturing the artist child that resides within us. I had been spending much effort and time on my art. The dream made me realize I wanted to show my friends (and myself) that I had resurrected my artist soul from the dusty attic of my being. Once I embraced this "baby" there was peace. I didn't want to loose this vivid imagery or the peace message, so I felt compelled to record it in an acrylic multi-media piece complete with cobwebs, sparkly lime glitter and a dreamy baby face.

The job of the artist

is always

to deepen the mystery.

FRANCIS BACON

Three Dimensional Exercises

Isabel in clay © Wewer Keohane

Keep in mind that there are many, many creative ways to honor your dream in the arts. Once you have done some of these exercises, your artist within will get excited and lead you on your personal journey expressing your vast creativity.

Paper Mache or Paper Clay can be fun, as can any form of clay. I find the paper clays to be easier to work with for simple shaping of dream symbols and that is what I would like you to do. Once you have the Mache mixed or the Paper clay opened, take a portion and form it into a symbol from one of your dreams. Pick a symbol that is still a mystery for you.....one that you know has deep meaning but that isn't a clear metaphor as of yet. (I keep a clump of super soft Sculpy next to where I watch TV and make a symbol a day.)
Make more than one of the same symbol so you can decorate, paint, and

view from all angles. Keep it by the bed, on your dashboard, or poke a hole from it and make a charm.

Draw it. Make a mobile out of several. Your Dreamer Within will be thrilled to be so honored that you can expect more dream activity to guide you once you do this. I have a mobile hanging in my studio made from an eclectic mix of dream symbols I have either made or found and it always gives me a charge to look up at it. No one will ever have a duplicate! This is the beauty of "arting" from dreams.

(Love and art are verbs, don't you know?)

Make a book honoring the dream and the symbol:

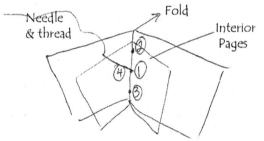

As shown in the 2-D section, make a carving of your symbol. Now, find a nice rice paper and print the carving on the right hand side of an 8.5" x 5.5" piece. Fold several sheets of 8.5" x 11" paper in half then in half again and fold the rice paper around it. Punch three small holes in the folds and sew thread through the holes starting in the middle. From the middle(1) go to an end hole(2) then to the other end hole(3) then back through the middle(4) and tie the thread together. You will have a small book or journal honoring your dream.

Here is Leslie's Book/Cover:

A great work of art is like a dream.
For all its apparent obviousness, it does not
explain itself and is never unequivocal.

Carl Jung

Poetry often enters
through the window
of irrelevance.

M.C. RICHARDS

CHAPTER FOUR

INSPIRED BY DREAMS:
LITERARY ARTS

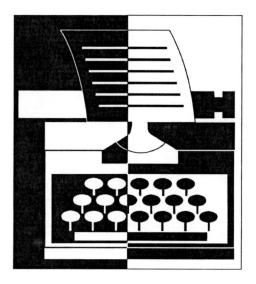

The Dream story itself is the most perfect
revelation of the truth of the dream.
Henry Reed, Ph.D.

The creative mind plays
with the objects it loves.

CARL JUNG

In 1993 I was asked by Doug Evans, director of the Colorado Mountain College Glenwood Writer's Conference, to do a workshop for writers. My theme would be "Inspired by Dreams". I began to collect works of other writers who had used their dreams as inspiration. Many synchronous happenings began.

I met Naomi Epel, author of <u>Writers Dreaming</u>, at an Association for the Study of Dreams conference where I was presenting. Her book became a source for the workshop. The one workshop turned into two, both very exciting and rewarding. I realized I wanted to continue the theme further, adding visual artists to the list of the inspired. I began teaching classes for anyone interested in unblocking or expanding their creativity. My first class was intimate and very rewarding. Many of the poems and Haiku through this book were written by those first participants. You will also see visual work, my own and others, from ongoing workshops and retreats.

All the Haiku used in this book were written in less than five minutes during class and were inspired by the dreams of the authors or dream material from other artists. They were strictly acts of spontaneous creativity. You might note a similar theme in some of the work because in the workshop we share each other's dreams as if they were our own (see Group section), and we all view the same dream-inspired work.

My deepest appreciation to Doug Evans for creating the opportunity for this new way of experiencing dreams, and to Steve, Barbie, Marcia and Martha for their courage and participation in my first workshop so many years ago, and to all the participants since.

What is not brought to consciousness
comes to us in fate.

CARL JUNG

Socrates' quote: "The unexamined life is not worth living." is especially applicable for writers because the unexamined life will lead to boring writing, and shallow manuscripts. The necessary cathartic writing done in the process of examining one's life is for our journals although it may offer great fodder for literary work and is necessary if we are to grow into our best selves. For me, the path of my life's examination, although it has had many routes, has had a main core led by dream work. I have been fascinated with dreams and writing since I was a child and have been keeping a dream journal for over 4 decades. When I first began to write, I wrote about how my dreams felt. Over the years I have learned, through dreamwork, how to embrace both the dark and light aspects of my psyche, and I would like to share with you how doing this work can not only greatly enhance your life, but your writing, whether it is prose, poetry, non-fiction or fiction.

As a writer, one of the most important skills is the ability to develop metaphor. Metaphor is the central theme of dreamwork. When you dream, you dream in symbols. It is convenient to say "my dream last night was because I ate pizza, or because I saw that Stephen King movie", but the truth is that whatever triggered the dream, the symbols are yours (and might not have a thing to do with the trigger). These are not King's symbols and even if they are food-induced, they are coming from **your** psyche.

met·a·phor [met-*uh*-fawr, -fer] noun

1. a figure of speech in which a term or phrase is applied to something to which it is not literally applicable in order to suggest a resemblance, as in "A mighty fortress is our God." Compare MIXED METAPHOR, SIMILE (def. 1).

2. something used, or regarded as being used, to represent something else; emblem; symbol.

source: dictionary.com

Each metaphor in your dream represents an aspect of yourself. So, if I dream of my mother, it is not my mother, but the aspect of self represented by mother that my sub-conscious is trying to show me.

As author Clive Barker says:

You don't even have to turn dreams into art.
For some people the whole idea of turning something into art is going to be a source of anxiety....But bringing it (the dream) kicking and squealing into the light and seeing the value of metaphor in your life, talking about the value of metaphor, that's what's important.

Metaphor works when examining life because it creates ownership of our material. When we learn to own our own material, we stop blaming, judging and projecting onto others. This creates compassion, empathy and joy within. We stop taking things personally.

How then, does it benefit your writing? For one, it stops the lecturing and cathartic kinds of writing that is better left in our journals. And, it gives us incredible material for character development and symbolism.

I find that after I have fully owned the metaphors in my dreams that I can then run amok with creativity and expression and have fun with the characters without being too closely connected to them. For instance, I had a dream about being tricked into a bathtub full of green water. No matter what I did, I could not get the green water off of me after that bath.

I asked myself how the dream made me feel, which is the first step I ask my dream clients to take with their dreams. Then I ask if it conjures any memories. In the green bath dream I felt bewildered and helpless to get the green off. It reminded me of an incident in college when a woman was enamored with my very long, at that time black, hair. She literally pestered me for weeks about how I grew it so long. Being young, fed up with her following me around, and not as kind as I am now, I told her I put Vaseline in my hair every night. She finally knew my secret, I told her. I don't know how I came up with that ridiculous idea, but it's what I told her. The next day she came to my dorm room devastated, her hair sticking up in spikes, no longer than the day before, begging me for the secret to getting the Vaseline out of her hair. I told her she had to use Cheer detergent. I don't know how well it worked, because she left me alone after that.

What does this memory have to do with the dream? For me, I finally got to feel, with this green all over my body, how this woman must have felt, all those years ago. The bathtub was a metaphor for my own sense of naiveté and helplessness. The green for envy. I don't remember today what I was feeling helpless about at the time of my dream, or why I was envious, but I remember I was able to associate my feeling with what was taking place in my life at the time. I also got to look at how badly I had wanted certain things and felt compassion for this young woman who envied and so badly wanted long hair.

After working with the dream, I felt a sense of self-forgiveness as well. I would never play a trick on someone like that today, and I was ashamed and embarrassed that I ever had. When the work on the dream was completed, I was able to use this woman as a character in a story I was writing. She became a metaphor for the longing in all of us to have things we deem important that in the long run are meaningless. Because I had experienced the dream, I had experienced the feelings, and I could build my character in the story much more thoroughly and believably.

Poet James Hall describes, in the book Writers Dreaming, by Naomi Epel, about the first poem he even published having been inspired by a dream. He felt the dream was like a visitation and he wrote the best poem he'd ever written to date. It took him years to write another poem as good. Later, when he began writing fiction, words would come to him in dreams.

There are many stories of great ideas coming in dreams. There are also great uses of dreams in novels which help unfold a character. One of my favorites is by M. Scott Peck, best known for The Road Less Traveled. Peck wrote a novel called A Bed by the Window in which one character's whole story unfolds through his dreams. The reader can feel Petri, the character, changing by witnessing his dream evolution. Allan Gurganus' short story, It Had Wings came directly from a dream experience.

Goethe's Faust and Stevenson's Dr. Jekyll and Mr. Hyde originated in dreams. Many portions of work by Tolstoy, Poe, Dante and Voltaire are known to have been inspired by their dreams. Further research will show story after story about the rich material honed from dreams and turned into great literature, fine art, music and film, as well as some of our greatest inventions. These dreamers were able to translate the metaphors in their dreams into masterpieces.

Metaphors are mirrors into ourselves. Seeing into the mirror will help you be accountable in your waking life and you will become free from any victim energy you may be carrying, or at least aware of it. Using metaphors as mirrors helps us embrace ourselves fully.

The strength of the metaphor is
its ability to express the inexpressible,
that is to communicate something
more vividly and forcefully
than by saying it directly.

The second aspect of dreamwork that can greatly benefit your writing is paradox. Paradox is a situation that defies intuition; a statement that leads to a contradiction; an apparent contradiction that actually expresses a non-dual truth. Our dreams are full of them!

par·a·dox [par-*uh*-doks] –noun

1. A statement or proposition that seems self-contradictory or absurd but in reality expresses a possible truth.

2. A self-contradictory and false proposition.

3. any person, thing, or situation exhibiting an apparently contradictory nature.

4. an opinion or statement contrary to commonly accepted opinion

source: dictionary.com

Paradox is holding the tension of the opposites. In fiction it might be seen as the conflict between the antagonist and the protagonist. Working with paradox in your dreams can give you great character material, needed tension and contrast.

Inwardly, paradox can take you out of the world of duality and polarized thinking into what Deepak Chopra calls the "unified field".

Emerson said, "true genius is the ability to understand metaphor and live in paradox and ambiguity". This means giving up judging whether things are good or bad and embracing them purely for what they are. This includes our emotions, other people, beliefs and ideas. Moving from judgment into discernment is necessary when working with paradox.

My belief is that we are all made up of everything: joy and grief, good and evil, etc. Because our society thinks and speaks in a dualistic language, it is very difficult to embrace and own what we have been taught as the "opposite" sides of ourselves.

In dreams, our shadow material will surface through the metaphors and the paradoxes within them. Nightmares, as discussed earlier, are often our subconscious trying desperately to get us to own this so called "dark" side of ourselves. Jung referred to the disowned parts of ourselves as our Shadow. You may refuse to own your beauty or your greed; either could be considered the shadow side of yourself. In our dreams, the shadow aspects reveal themselves to us. The dream helps us to integrate these parts of ourselves that we refuse to see in ourselves, but are usually quick to see in others.

In our society many people pretend that evil only exists outside themselves. Unless we own the parts of ourselves that we are projecting on others, we will never be whole. Exploring our dreams can help us embrace the parts of ourselves we have been judging so harshly. We can then drop judgment of others, and build some great dark characters from what we have learned.

On more than one occasion, a dreamer has dreamed of a "pair of ducks". A great metaphor and play on words for paradox!

Pair of Ducks photo by D. Evans

This is a good time to show how some dreamers have brought their dream experiences to writing. I call this dream empathy. Your quality of life will greatly improve when you are able to have empathy for yourself and others. The quality of your writing is enhanced by the experiences in your dreams that would never occur in waking life.

em·pa·thy [em-puh-thee] –noun

1. the intellectual identification with or vicarious experiencing of the feelings, thoughts, or attitudes of another.

2. the imaginative ascribing to an object, as a natural object or work of art, feelings or attitudes present in oneself: *By means of empathy, a great painting becomes a mirror of the self.*

source: dictionary.com

For instance, Ann Rice made a decision to give her vampires the gift of flight. How could she really write well about flying when she'd never flown? You probably guessed it - by flying in her dreams. She asked for dreams of flight and she received them. In the morning after a flight dream she would write down every detail of her flight. Voila, flying vampires that seem realistic because Rice had the experience of flight. Dreams give us an added benefit of experience.

My friend Rita learned to roller skate backwards in her dreams. I speak French in my dreams and have to hurriedly write down the words when I wake up and look them up since in conscious life I have a limited vocabulary. In my dreams, my accent is perfect because in my dreams I speak French perfectly.

What have you done in your dreams that you have not done in your waking life that can add authenticity to your writing? Think about dreams that gave you an otherworldly experience and write from that, or at least write a detailed explanation of the episode and file it away for future reference.

Inspired by dreams exercises:

One of the most playful ways to make art from your dreams is to see your dreams as stories, plays, poems, films or vignettes. Take any symbol from your dream (some of the best stories come from bringing life to inanimate objects within the dream – think Tom Robbins) and give the symbol a life of its own, separate from the dream.

1. Titles: Simply giving your dream a title can provide a creative jolt. It can also produce amazing insight into the meaning of the dream. On mornings that you can't devote the required time to really play with a dream, just title it. You might be pleasantly surprised by what you are shown. Between the felt sense of the dream and titling the dream can come an amazing awareness of the dream's message and depth.

2. Haiku: In the morning, after feeling into your dream, write a short poem or Haiku. A Haiku is a three line poem with five syllables in the first and third lines and seven syllables in the second line. For example:

Feather on a walk
Blue with fringe of red and black
Where does the bird fly?

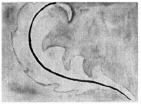

Flight© Wewer Keohane

A Haiku will often reveal the deep meaning of your dream. Illustrate your haiku to awaken your visual artist within. This creates ownership of your symbols as did the association exercise in chapter two.

3. Poetry: extend your Haiku theme into a full fledged poem as below. First, rent Kurasawa's Dreams from the video store. Alone, or with a group, watch each of the dreams, doing a Haiku from each, then put them together for a poem:

Wing-loosed color lays
on green-felted ground
* sun plays.*
dancing yet
* in breeze*

Though time may ravage
* what is loved*
* is never lost.*
Heart in dream
* dies not.*

Mind fields complex
* above spirals*
* to*
*   below.*
Gentle healing space.

Fox's rainbow path
his mother
*   tempts child to man.*
Not man,
* not child now.*

Black angel of death
* you carry me*
*   between*
*   worlds*
never looking back.

Vincent's connection
eye to heart
* moves*
* hand to brush*
fire
* air*
*   water*
*   earth.*

Steve K.

77

4. Journaling: If you just start writing about how you feel after a dream, what the dream triggers might have been, and relate them to some childhood memory you can develop some great short story material. This combines your personal work with your imaginative abilities and will move you and your story telling forward.

5. Dialogue: Have your symbols talk with each other and with you. I like to write with my dominant hand when it's my voice and the non-dominant hand when it is the voice of a symbol. This is a playful way to discover the personality of your characters and symbols.

6. Details for storytelling: The more detail you write about from the dream, the more it will build your skill as a writer. If you find you are being lazy, what does this say about your ability to build a plot, develop a character? Try to remember and record every last detail in your dream. Some people discover they have a complete story from the dream when they begin to record all of it.

Start now by writing a short story using a symbol or character from your latest dream. Let go and be playful.

Here are some helpful ways to start:
Character Development:

Character's name_____
Sex __Age_____
Physical appearance: body type, hair, eyes, facial features, dress, posture, movements, mannerisms, speech, first impression, ...

Background influences: education, religion, family, early childhood experiences, financial situation, habits, health, history, profession, marital status, other relationships, addictions, sexual preferences, environments.

The inner person: distinctive traits, self image, yearnings/dreams, fears apprehensions, sense of humor, code of ethics, attitude, night dreams.

Other details: hobbies, favorite foods, hated foods, favorite books, movies, music, art.

Positive traits:

Negative traits:

Why was this person in your dream?
Your hero or your demise?
Have you allowed yourself to get outrageously creative with this character? Have you given yourself permission to bring life to an inanimate object? Why or why not?

 NOW........take all this information and write your story!
Begin here:

TITLE:

STORY:

Listening is a form
of acceptance.

S.T. MANN

CHAPTER FIVE

SHARING THE PROCESS

The King's Napkin © Wewer Keohane

GROUP WORK

To live a creative life, we must
lose our fear of being wrong.

JOSEPH CHILTON PEARCE

In the early eighties, while earning my Ph.D., I developed a group process for dreamwork, inspired by working with Dr. Montague Ullman. This process is included in the following pages. I hope the process will encourage you to form a group with others so inclined. The individual exercises found elsewhere in the book can also be done as a group, as can the visual and literary art exercises.

I have also had great success using this process in business retreats by replacing dreams with personal problems. The participants, rather than contribute a dream, offer a problem anonymously by writing it down and placing it in a bowl. Another individual in the group draws from the bowl and takes the problem on as his own. From that point on, the rules of my dream process are enforced. After your read the following pages, you will understand how and why this works so beautifully.

As I said in the introduction, nothing beats the workshop experience, but I hope the following words convey my devotion to the work and to you, the dreamer, enough to inspire you in the way a workshop could.

May you have the courage to allow your dreams to awaken your authentic Self, for an authentic life is the greatest form of worship.

It always comes back to the same necessity:
go deep enough and there is a bedrock of truth.

MAY SARTON

Developing a Dream Workshop

This is the handout I use for the group training process in my dream workshops. The workshop is designed to explore why people dream, and what dreams mean. It centers on the layperson being able to understand dreams without the help of a professional. Participants come to the workshop with at least one short dream (recent dreams if possible). They also bring lots of paper, their dream journal if they have one, pencils and a sense of curiosity and courage.

Purposes of this process:
To help participants remember and understand their dreams.
To better understand the creativity and metaphors in dreams.
To better understand "felt sense" as it differs from emotion while honoring the emotion of the dream.
To emphasize that the ultimate authority for the meaning of the dream is the dreamer and that the dream story itself if far more important than the interpretation.
To encourage therapists to do dreamwork with their clients.
To encourage the formation of dream groups using this technique.

To educate students of psychology on the importance of dreams and give them the ability to work with dreams in their future careers.

To have fun with the mystery, metaphors and mirrors presented in our dreams.

To grow into an integrated being with reverence for the dreamer within and life itself.

To increase the understanding that working with dreams is not about being clever, but about being intuitive and trusting the felt sense.

Before you begin your workshop, there are some necessary clarifications:

Metaphor:

There is a sense of metaphor about a dream. Therefore, when we are dreaming, we are artists, poets, creating new metaphors which relate to our life as an art form. We have to deal with the function of working with our dreams in a waking state, so we are left with feelings and verbal explanations. It is sometimes confusing, like trying to describe the experience of awe upon seeing a painting masterpiece, or hearing a poem that moves you. (See Working Alone section.)
There is a difference of expression because of the social purpose of language. In sleeping we use a pictorial image like animals might. We humanize this ability and change the primitive symbols by making them into metaphors, coming up with a combination of pictures, dreams, life positions. For instance, we may dream of a car without brakes going downhill, a metaphor for feeling out of control.

Healing:

1. The emotional atmosphere or "residue" stays with us from the previous 24-48 hours or more. While sleeping we are not taking in any new information but we use the sleep time to program with

bits and pieces and to open our remote memory system which is connected to our emotional state of the present.

2. Dreams can also help us take an historical view of our lives without consciously remembering the history. Dreams are a potentially healing instrument because they are connected with the unfinished business of the past. They are also a connection to the Divine Source.

> We do not dream what we
> already know consciously.

3. Asleep and dreaming we are alone and we risk taking a profound look at who we really are, by our concept of truth. Work must be done in the waking state in order for dreams to be fully used for healing and emotional growth. Dreams are the pearls of oysters. We produce them alone (with the help of the Divine, that is!). They are "accidental" as are pearls. We enclose the event and if we do not use it, we cannot make a pearl necklace. The grit is the gem.

This is not to say that dreams don't heal us without our participation. They do. By pushing us forward with their cleansing properties even without our participation, we are often healed or prepared for the future.

The Talmud states: A dream not understood is like a letter not opened. I would change "understood" to "felt".... A dream not felt is like a letter not opened.

Problems

1. Because in dreams we are poets, speaking a metaphoric language, we often write our dreams off as interesting but silly, and anything but healing. Think of how often you've heard someone say, "It was the pizza I ate last night." when justifying a wild dream.

2. Awake we are once again actors in the social scene and using our clever ways (ego) to prevent us from clear truth about ourselves. It is harder to take an honest look at ourselves through our dreams than it is to write our dreams off as a silly relaxing release not worthy of being taken seriously.

It is not easy to fully realize what the dream is saying by yourself. This can cause a dilemma for the self because we, on one hand, want to know the full meaning of our dreams, and on the other hand, have a fear of what the true meaning may be. When we develop the courage to face the intimate aspects of our psyche we begin to want more and more answers to use for growth and healing. This is where other people interested in developing the same courage and change can come into the picture.

What do dreamers need from others to help them understand their dreams?

1. The dreamer needs to know that s/he is safe and will not be hurt. This must be voluntarily shared with the group and upheld at all cost. Deep feelings need a loving environment to flourish.

2. The dreamer needs to know that no one will push her beyond the point of disclosure that s/he wants – this power must stay in the hands of the dreamer, who can stop at any time he or she wants. The dreamer needs help in understanding safety and discovery. The group must be sensitive to the dreamer. As

dreamers, we are like fish trying to get back into water. If the group is caring, unbelievable creativity and growth can take place, which, of course, leads to incredible healing, not just for the dreamer of the moment, but for the whole group.

What is the role of the team leader?

The leader insures integrity of process and safety of the dreamer and participates as all other members of the group. Should guidelines be crossed, the team leader gently brings the group back to the safety point. In no way should the leader act as an authority, pretending as if they know the meaning of the dream.

How do you begin?

1. I recommend the participants commit to six week sessions. The team leader – who could be different each meeting, (drawing names from a hat every few weeks will work) asks, "Does anyone have a dream they would like to share?"
2. Do not ask, "Did anyone have a dream?" There is usually already enough urge to take the risk of sharing. The risk comes in sharing and saying out loud the dream you volunteer to share. Sometimes by simply stating the

dream out loud, one gains new insight. The benefit of risk!

The group will close their eyes, make the dream their own and allow it to evoke in themselves the feelings it would as if they had just dreamed the dream. This includes giving the dream personal feeling first.

They share their feelings with the group. This is one of the most important guidelines:

As you share your feelings of the dream, always speak as if it was your dream, i.e., "in my dream". Never give advice, nor say "you", or "your dream is about".......

In this stage, the group is developing metaphoric meaning and it is crucial to the safety and vulnerability of the Dreamer who offered the dream that no one project their interpretation on him or her. *This is the crux of this system and will guarantee safety in the group.*

Most members will slip up and say "you", or do some sort of projection such as "One of the women is probably your mother." The team leader gently says to this person: "Say, I, or in my dream, or say, in my dream the older woman represents my mother."

I cannot stress enough how important this guideline is. As an example: In a recent workshop one of the dreamers kept saying "you" instead of "in my dream". I gently corrected her and when the work was done I asked if she would mind hearing from the Dreamer how it felt in both situations......hearing "you" versus hearing "in my dream" from this participant. She wanted to learn so she asked the Dreamer how it felt and the Dreamer simply stated: When I heard "you" I felt punched. When I heard "in my dream" I felt I had a choice to accept the information or not. I did not feel judged.

So....after hearing the dream spoken, each person in the group pretends this is his or her dream. Henceforth, the dream is spoken of in the first person. We may not say to a dreamer who has dreamed about two women: "One of the women is your sister." We can say, "In my dream, one of the women is my sister."

This makes the dream our own and the dreamer has the choice of deciding if the information we have shared is pertinent to her dream or not.

As the dreamer relates her dream to the group, each individual in the group writes down the dream. The dreamer must relay the dream slowly and articulately. We then have something to refer to when we make the dream our own. (After many months of a group meeting together, the writing down becomes less necessary, except for particularly complex dreams.) After writing the dream, ask the Dreamer to repeat the dream so everyone can close their eyes and imagine dreaming the dream themselves.

We then take turns expressing how having this dream has made us feel. After this, we touch base with the dreamer. Then we take turns expressing metaphors for "our" dream. This includes "owning" all the symbols as parts of ourselves. After this we again touch base with the dreamer.

Why should this process work?

According to most analysts, it shouldn't work! But it does. Why? Because the same emotions touch us all, we just have different history to apply to the emotions. The process works in subtle ways. Shared psyche enables us to go deeper into our own psyche. Each of us is trying to get in touch with our issues and the implications of our issues through our dreams. When we hear what issues and implications our dream raises in others, it gives us confidence to continue the work.

After each step of the dream work, the dreamer is invited to say where s/he is with the dream now and s/he should be given all the time needed. Also, if at any time a dreamer wants to stop the process, the group must agree. (This proves to be very rare.)

At the end of the session it is important to dialogue with the dreamer and the group. This develops the experience and the skills, but it is necessary to start the dialogue in the beginning. Ask the dreamer to tell the group what s/he has discovered about their dream during the process. This allows closure.

Guidelines:

If the dreamer has not identified the life issue of why they might have had the dream that night, then ask questions regarding the emotional clime of the dreamer when s/he went to bed. Also, ask for what the dreamer considers to be their "triggers" in the previous 24-48 hour period. In other words......does this dream remind you of anything that has recently happened in your waking life...either literally, or in a felt sense.

If the imagery is not clear to the dreamer, help build these questions for the dreamer. Tell the dreamer that these are instruments for their use and they should answer or not answer, but use the questions to explore and share only what they decide. Remember, the more the dreamer shares, the more the dreamer learns.

Never ask a leading question because you are giving the dreamer your personal interpretation when you do so. Remember, interpretations are individual and one of the rules of this system is to honor individual interpretation and feelings.

For instance, don't ask: "Is one of those women your mother?", but rather, ask; "Why do you think you put an elderly woman dream, the elderly woman represents the mother part of myself, which is....."

We must get over our need to be a dream interpreter for other people. This will help us also in daily life to accept other people as they are rather than trying to change them into clones of ourselves or the selves we wish we were.

Develop the following skills of listening when hearing a dreamer speak. Listen for:

> Emphasis and feeling;
> Roles of the characters;
> Themes;
> Words (especially ones with double meaning, i.e. "pair of ducks" aka paradox);
> Repetitions;
> What isn't said;
> Changes in tone of voice.

> To what extent the dreamer has identified why they had the dream that night, i.e., have they shared possible triggers for the dream? Have you and the dreamer owned the symbols in the dream as aspects of yourselves? (See story in last section of the book about my radio show.)

Give the dreamer the credence to come up with heir own interpretation – the ability to develop the art of coming up with questions. And, above all, honor how the dream makes the dreamer and other participants **feel**.

The Process of Individual Interpretation:

1. After a dream has been shared fully (we have said how it makes us feel, and we have developed metaphors), we try to develop the immediate context from what the dreamer dreamed:
   a. What were their last thoughts before going to bed?
   b. What encounters with people did they have during the day?
   c. Can the dreamer find likenesses within himself that remind him of the characters in the dream?

Simply help the dreamer reconstruct the day to enrich their life context. We put too little meaning in how we felt throughout the day. This will help us realize the importance of all moments.

2. Call the dreamer's attention to every scene and element in their dream. Go over one scene at a time and have the dreamer look at it from an elaborated context of questioning each element, one at a time.

3. Discuss the metaphor ideas that came up before we knew any of the dreamer's thoughts. The dreamer plays back some of the ideas of the group as an integrative projection (since it is now filtered back through the dreamer's psyche) and the dreamer takes only what may relate to their dream. Has everyone in the group "owned" the symbols?

4. It is amazing how hearing what our dream **doesn't** mean to us, but to someone else, can clarify what the dream **does** mean to us.

5. Suggest to the dreamer that they take a look at their own dream again before the group meets again. At the beginning of the next meeting, the last dream worked on can be briefly discussed.

Remember, this method relies on metaphors and feelings, not on interpretation. It is based on each of us having our own set or sets of symbols and that there are not universal "right" answers to any one dream. Remember to create an environment where defenses are not necessary.

Congratulations on having the courage to learn the meaning of and to feel the messages of your dreams. The self understanding that will come through this process will truly enhance your life and bring you great comfort.

May your work remind you that you are connected to the Divine, worthy and rich with depth. One with the Source.

Until we accept the fact
that life itself is founded in mystery,
we shall learn nothing.

HENRY MILLER

I would love to know of groups formed and using this process via wewerart.com.

CHAPTER SIX

PERSONAL SYMBOLS

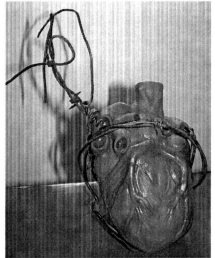

His Heart Was Wrapped in Barbed Wire © Wewer Keohane

Most of the symbols in this section are from the carvings
in my original Dream Art Workbook,
with the amazing help and digital transformation by my
talented husband, Steve.

Trust in yourself.
Your perceptions are often far more accurate
than you are willing to believe.

CLAUDIA BLACK

Dreamer........you are the author of
your dreams. Therefore, please don't refer
to a symbol book for the meaning of your
dreams. Instead, go back to the exercises
in this book and find the *personal* meaning.
Then, record that meaning in the symbol
section which follows on the next pages.
Over the years you may find the meanings of
your symbols make interesting alterations.
It has been my experience that they
continue to repeat themselves in our
personal iconography.
Once you make recording yours a habit, you
may be surprised by how often many of them
repeat themselves and how creative your
personal metaphors are.
Dreams help us honor our creativity.
Enjoy your unique symbol book.
I hope you will create art, write stories and
develop a truly authentic life
because of this work.

Every child is an artist.
The problem is how to remain an artist once
he grows up.

PABLO PICASSO

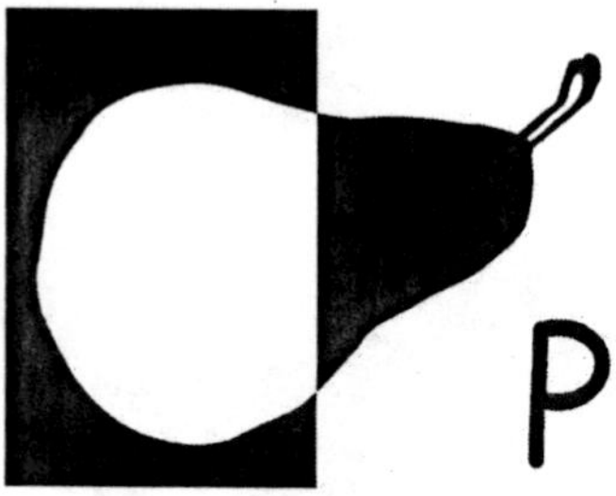

Artful Dreaming by Wewer Keohane

CHAPTER SEVEN

Stories, Endorsements & Testimonials

Evolution (front) © Wewer Keohane

Thanks to everyone who has written to me regarding my work and **Artful Dreaming**. I wish I could print all the letters and emails. Each is dear to my heart

Is a dream ever finished
or does it just stop
in interesting places?

This book has changed my life by giving me everyday tools to access and understand the visions of the universe within, gifted to me every night in my dreams.
DOUG EVANS, Writer, Artist, Gardener

One of my favorite memories of dreamwork comes from a radio show I did in Aspen, Colorado in the mid eighties.   A caller told of his dream of being afraid to jump from an airplane. Not an odd fear for most of us, but he was a frequent jumper. So I asked him if there was something else he was afraid to "jump into". He gasped, laughed, and said," I have been wanting to ask my girlfriend to marry me and I am afraid she might say no." His girlfriend was listening and called in to say "yes". Wewer

I love going into the schools and doing mini workshops with fourth graders and above to introduce them to dream work.   This letter is a thank you for one of those workshops:

Dear Dr. Wewer,

Thank you for coming to tell us about dreams. I thought that you told us some of the neatest things I have ever heard in my life. I really didn't know anything that you told us and I never knew that anything like what you told us could really happen. I never dreamed of it but now I know now and I will know forever. I don't know how much to thank you for doing what you did for us but thank you thank you thank you.

Good Bye and thank you again!
Sincerely, Elizabeth, Fourth Grader

When my cousin, Tyler, died, I was only eight, but I remember the family said every time we saw an eagle that it was Tyler. So I'd wave at every eagle I saw. My Grandfather just died and I really miss him, but I did

have a dream where I am asleep on a cloud. In the dream, I wake up and on the cloud above me is an eagle and I know it is Tyler and I smile. Then a much larger eagle flies in and sits next to Tyler so the two eagles are on the cloud looking down at me and I know it is my Grandpa and Tyler and I felt really peaceful.
IvAnn Dickerson, 6th Grade Artist

At 74 years old I attended my first dream workshop with Wewer. I went to observe (& probably judge) something new and perhaps scary to me. I expected nothing much, just some entertainment, perhaps. I hadn't recorded a dream as requested so I worked with a childhood dream. No expectations. As the process proceeded, I felt huge energy – ah hah – blink! – and I knew absolutely what this painting I had hidden and wondered about actually was. The boogie man in my childhood dream had scared me all my life. Now it was art on the paper. Gone forever. I haven't missed a workshop since! I need to include how absolutely charged I got and the continued highs I get when I venture into dreams - Wewer it is opening up so much more to who I am, was, and will be. Have I found the source everyone seems to write about?
Ellen Zagoras, Artist

In Wewer's world, every event is cause for celebration and rarely does an object, inanimate or otherwise, escape her always successful effort to improve its appearance. She is warm, intelligent, generous, sensitive to a fault, terminally optimistic, and easily the most creative person I've ever had the pleasure of knowing. EVERYTHING she touches is improved!
Neal Pollack, Master Goldsmith/Computer Consultant/ Philosopher/ Social Commentator

136

Hi Wewer -I wanted to tell you how much I enjoyed coming to see you and hear your words of wisdom. I do appreciate and value your teaching - it is marvelous that this opportunity has arrived to the planet!
Andrea Metz, Artist and Web Designer

Wewer takes many ideas, often with an obscure common denominator, and distills them into a few words or simple visual statement that hits the mark so the rest of us can cut through the clutter and "get it." Her book art with the clamps, the heart w/barbed wire, are examples of this. It is so natural to her that she doesn't even know she is doing it......that's a gift!!!!!! Wewer is as unique as her name. Because she is open to uncertainty, she doesn't become locked into artistic dogma, or the dreary dead habits that limit human potentials. Her gift to us is that because she respects others as they are and also honors their potential, she is able to foster that self discovery and liberation in us as well.
Patty Ringer, Certified Master Porcelain Artist/Teacher

Dear Wewer, It is my absolute pleasure to be able to attend these dream workshops. Never would I have imagined I would receive such a blessing. I was serendipitously led to a workshop during a pivotal point in my life full of profound transformation. In sharing at the very first workshop I attended, I was shown the healing power of my dream and felt relief, awareness, acceptance and joy!

Because this process is intuitive, the wisdom of the entire universe is accessible to each and every one of us. I have returned to my higher self, who was always waiting for me, and come into my soul work. I believe it is not only possible, but imperative that humanity return to its union with spirit, in which ever way works.

My intention is to continue on this path and share it with others. I want to thank you again for the gift of the workshops. I am so amazed and fortunate to have come to my dreams as well as my artist, and experience the power, guidance, and mystery of it all.

With most sincere gratitude
Loni Tervol , Artist

One of the gifts I most admire in Wewer Keohane is her amazing ability to fluently travel within and between the worlds of dreams and art. Her expertise as well as her passion will deeply inspire as you allow her to be your guide into this journey of authentic self-expression and self-discovery. Enjoy.
Gayle Lukeman, MA, LMFT and co-author of *Beyond Blame: Reclaiming the Power You Give to Others.*

May your dreams
be blessed
for loving
this book.

Please share your dreams
and art from dreams with me
via www.wewerart.com
or
theartfuldreamer.blogspot.com

2836440